NEXT ROUND

A YOUNG ATHLETE'S JOURNEY TO GOLD

JOHN SPRAY

pajamapress

www.pajamapress.ca   info@pajamapress.ca

 Canada Council   Conseil des arts
for the Arts   du Canada

ONTARIO ARTS COUNCIL
CONSEIL DES ARTS DE L'ONTARIO
an Ontario government agency
un organisme du gouvernement de l'Ontario

Canadä

The publisher gratefully acknowledges the support of the Canada Council for the Arts and the Ontario Arts Council for its publishing program. We acknowledge the financial support of the Government of Canada through the Canada Book Fund (CBF) for our publishing activities.

Library and Archives Canada Cataloguing in Publication
Spray, John, 1948-, author
  Next round : a young athlete's journey to gold / John Spray.
Includes index.
ISBN 978-1-77278-003-1 (hardback).--ISBN 978-1-77278-001-7 (paperback)
 .1. Biyarslanov, Arthur, 1995- --Juvenile literature. 2. Boxers (Sports)--
Canada--Biography--Juvenile literature. I. Title.
GV1132.B59S67 2016   j796.83092   C2016-900258-6

Publisher Cataloging-in-Publication Data (U.S.)
Names: Spray, John R., author.
Title: Next round / John Spray.
Description: Toronto, Ontario Canada : Pajama Press, 2016. | Includes index.| Summary: "Arthur Biyarslanov fled war in Chechnya as a child, ultimately coming to Canada as a refugee. Thriving on the challenge and discipline of sport, he won gold for Canada at the 2015 Pan Am Olympic Games, bringing him a step closer to qualifying for the 2016 Summer Olympic Games. Written from extensive interviews with Arthur and his family, Next Round includes photographs, an index, and a glossary"— Provided by publisher.
Identifiers: ISBN 978-1-77278-003-1 (hardcover) | ISBN 978-1-77278-001-7 (pbk.)
Subjects: LCSH: Biyarslanov, Arthur – Juvenile literature. | Boxers (Sports) -- Biography – Juvenile literature. | ·
Sports -- Biography – Juvenile literature. | Refugees – Chechnia (Russia) – Juvenile literature. | BISAC: JUVENILE NONFICTION / Biography & Autobiography / Sports & Recreation. | JUVENILE NONFICTION / Sports & Recreation / Olympics. | JUVENILE NONFICTION / Social Issues / Emigration & Immigration.
Classification: LCC GV1132.B5S673 |DDC 796.830922 – dc23

Cover and book design—Rebecca Buchanan
Front Cover Photo—"Pan Am men's boxing final" © 2016 Richard Lautens/GetStock.com. Back Cover Photo—
"Arthur wears his Pan Am gold medal" © Rick Bender. Other images courtesty of the Biyarslanov family

Manufactured by Friesens
Printed in Canada

Pajama Press Inc.
181 Carlaw Ave. Suite 207 Toronto, Ontario Canada, M4M 2S1

Distributed in Canada by UTP Distribution
5201 Dufferin Street Toronto, Ontario Canada, M3H 5T8

Distributed in the U.S. by Ingram Publisher Services
1 Ingram Blvd. La Vergne, TN 37086, USA

TABLE OF CONTENTS

FOR ALL THOSE CHILDREN who escaped the horrors of war to find peace and new beginnings...and for Arthur, who replaced the sound of gunfire with the smack of leather on a punching bag.—J.S.

Chechen civilians wait behind
a wall of Russian soldiers

CHAPTER 1

THE RUSSIAN SOLDIERS had completely blockaded the end of the bridge going into Dagestan. There were huge, battle-scarred tanks, muddy artillery pieces, rocket-propelled grenade launchers and Russian-made Kalashnikov rifles. Most of the soldiers were combat-hardened veterans who had fought in the first Chechen war. Their expressions blank, they stared quietly at the crowd of refugees on the bridge. The refugees stared back at the fierce-looking soldiers and their weaponry, wondering what to do next. A bomber flew high over the bridge with a fighter-jet escort. A few seconds later, the sounds of heavy explosions came from the city of Gudermes, the hometown they and thousands of other refugees had just left.

"Nana," three-year-old Arthur Biyarslanov said, pulling on his mother's coat. "Nana." He was afraid and confused, and tears pooled in his nut-brown eyes.

"There...there," Alla cooed, patting her son's head. "Soon it will be okay. Soon we will have sweet tea and cake."

A heavily armed helicopter gunship, bristling with rockets and machine guns, circled and dipped over the bridge like an angry bird of prey, its growling motor and *whap-whap* blades drowning out his mother's words. Arthur began to cry in earnest. His twelve-year-old sister, Bariyat, knelt to comfort him.

A Russian helicopter downed by Chechen militants near the capital Grozny, during the First Chechen War

NEXT ROUND

"I'm going to talk to the soldiers," Arthur's mother yelled over the whirring sound of the gunship, "I think they'll let a mother and four children across. You two—," she said, pointing to Bariyat and Arthur's nine-year-old brother, Rustam. "You take care of our little wolf. I'll take Bella with me to talk with the soldiers. She has the face of an angel. It will calm their dark hearts."

Alla and eleven-year-old Bella walked slowly across the bridge. It was three o'clock in the afternoon on a bright, sunny, but bitterly cold October day. Bella bravely watched their shadows glide across the floor of the bridge. She was afraid to look at the soldiers. Alla and Bella's hands were raised high above their heads and Alla frantically waved a white handkerchief. When they had come within twenty yards of the Russians, an older officer in a heavy woolen greatcoat and fur hat picked up a megaphone. "Stop right now!" he barked in Russian. "One more step and we will shoot you for sure...we will...okay, ladies?...all of us will and that's for sure. Okay? Go back now...Okay?"

The three children left behind held hands and watched in terror. "Nana! Nana! Come back, Nana. I'm hungry, Nana," Arthur sobbed.

That morning, on the slow bus ride from their home to the bridge, they had passed a herd of cattle, huddled tightly together to stay warm in the sub-zero cold. Great clouds of foggy steam escaped from the cows' nostrils as they breathed out in the icy air. "Look, Arthur," Bella had joked, "those cows are smoking cigarettes." Everyone, even the stern-faced Alla, had laughed at this. Now the children's eyes fixed on the soldiers. They saw again the pillows of steam, but this time coming not from sleepy cattle but from the tight knot of armed soldiers. The soldiers exhaled rapidly, steam puffing out ever more quickly. The soldiers were nervous with anticipation, knowing that something was about to happen. They'd been there before and could smell what was coming in the air.

Members of the Russian army in Chechnya in 1995

A very young soldier, perhaps only seventeen, was not breathing hard. He was sitting on top of the tank next to the turret, armed with a sniper's rifle. He wore neither hat nor helmet as he squinted through the high optic lens of his scope, his long golden hair blowing in the cold Caucasus wind. He kept both eyes open, as his grandfather had taught him as a boy hunting deer in Belarus. He fingered the trigger with his forefinger and breathed in slow, shallow breaths. None of this was new. He had the face of a choir boy...a soprano whose voice had yet to change. His hard, steely gray eyes said something else. This boy looked at Alla through his scope.

"No...no, you must listen," Alla yelled. "I am a mother with four young children. We mean you no harm. We only want passage through Dagestan to reach Azerbaijan. We are only a family...we are not insurgents."

The 120 or so people on the bridge behind her were also not insurgents. They were only desperate families weary of war and wanting to flee to any land free of bombs and bullets. There were some cars stuffed with refugees on the bridge, but mostly the people were on foot. They were normal families—fathers and mothers, pipe-smoking grandpas, children of all ages, and wailing babies. They dragged along overstuffed suitcases and roped bundles of clothing. One old woman carried a sewing machine, hoping for seamstress work once in Azerbaijan. A very tall, muscular young man toted a heavy box of his plumbing tools. A small girl had hidden her orange kitten under her coat, shushing it and trying to stop it from mewing. There was a small, scruffy dog on the bridge, belonging to no one, looking for handouts.

"You must let us through. We are just a mother and her children." Alla took a step forward.

The Russian officer had heard the stories...had read the bulletins from headquarters. The Mujahedeen, whose foreign fighters had entered Dagestan to help tear the republic from Mother Russia, would send in women and children, wearing vests of explosives. The officer looked at Alla and Bella, the woman and girl dressed in layers of sweaters and woolen overcoats, and wondered what sort of nasty plastic explosives lay beneath. He tossed the megaphone to the side, grabbed a Kalashnikov from the young soldier next to him, and fired a long burst of warning shots, the bullets skipping along the concrete floor of the bridge at Alla's side. Alla and Bella turned and ran for their lives. The young sniper slowly exhaled and took his finger off the trigger.

One nervous and anxious young soldier suddenly began firing without orders, startling himself. Then the other soldiers also raised their rifles and fired into the crowd. Their swarm of bullets sang and whizzed and stung like a mob of angry wasps. Then came the rocket-propelled grenades and artillery shells and a raspy rattling from above as the gunship made its voice heard. Arthur, Rustam, and Bariyat were frozen with fear as the people on the bridge ran in all directions...or fell down to the cold, hard cement.

"Nana," Arthur whispered. "Nana?"

Russian troops in Gudermes, Chechnya

CHAPTER 2

THERE WAS MASS PANIC and terror as the people ran from the bridge. Arthur could hear the screams and the noise of explosions all around him as his brother dragged him under a car, followed by Bariyat, where Rustam thought they would be safe. Debris flew through the air, striking the car, and then a rocket hit the car parked in front of them, releasing a fountain of fire and smoke and a deadly rain of glass and sharp sheets of hot metal. Rustam pulled Arthur out from under the car and ran beside his sister from the bridge, tripping on the broken box and the plumber's scattered tools. Rustam was a strong nine-year-old, but he could not carry his brother, especially when Arthur was wrapped up in a cocoon of woolens to ward off the cold weather.

The uniformed Chechen border police were on the Chechen side of the bridge. Seeing Rustam's attempts to hurry Arthur along, one of the border guards picked up the little boy and began to run with him to the "safe zone" in the Chechen woods. "What's your name?" he asked, looking down at Arthur cradled in his arms. Arthur had long been given the nickname of *Borz*...Chechen for wolf. "Ah," the border policeman laughed, "We can't have anything happen to the *Noxchi Borz*"...the Chechen Wolf. Bariyat and Rustam ran beside them.

"Where's Nana?" Rustam asked her. "Have you seen Bella?" Bariyat, already out of breath and in shock, only shook her head. Tears streamed down her face and she sobbed softly.

The bridge behind them was carpeted with the dead, the dying, and the wounded. Thirty-five dead and many more injured. The refugees' belongings lay scattered about: clothing, exploded suitcases, a clock-radio...and a sewing machine. The small dog, unhurt, ran in circles, temporarily deaf from the explosions. A beefy Russian walked to him, picked him up, and gave him some sweet, dried meat from his shirt pocket. The dog walked across the bridge to hang about the Russians.

The Chechen border police passed Arthur from man to man as they ran with him. His two siblings kept up, but all were tired and hungry. They had awoken early to leave their

15

home in Gudermes and were in shock from the violence of the day's emotionally charged events. They jogged and ran to the forest and the "safe zone" designated by the Russians. They and scores of other refugees huddled there. But Nana and Bella were not among them.

"I don't like it here, Rustam," said Arthur. And Bariyat, cold and hungry as the sun began to set, nodded her head in agreement.

"We will take you to the village of Qirzel," said the men. "There are people there that will take you in. It is still a long way...almost four miles, but we must hurry. Your mother and sister will find you there...hopefully."

"Where's my Nana?" Arthur demanded, "Where's my cake?"

The woods were dark, and as they jogged along, the forest became thicker. The huge stands of oak and the shivering beeches, their leaves clacking in the cold wind, crowded in on them. Rustam recalled the stories about the leopards, bears, and snarly, gray wolves that lived in the woods. "Never go into the deep woods alone!" his grandfather had cautioned him. "Little boys go in...they don't come out." Now Rustam began to cry. He wished his mother were there with him.

Others who had escaped the horrors of the bridge also ran through the forest. Two ten-year-old twin girls trotted alongside a chubby but surprisingly agile grandmother, her bright yellow apron bouncing off her thick knees as she

Chechen refugees on the long walk from Gudermes

scampered over rotting logs and through brambles. She sang an old Chechen folk song in a loud, falsetto warble. The twins giggled. The muscular plumber limped by, one pant leg ripped. He carried a crying toddler in his arms while the young, wounded mother rode piggyback. "Bad soldiers. Bad soldiers," the mother repeated again and again to anyone who might listen.

After hours of jogging and tripping through the dense woods, Arthur's little group came at last to the small village of Qirzel. The friendly smell of the wood stoves and the brightly lit little houses made the children smile. It all looked safe and warm. The border guard put Arthur down and knocked on a door. The old couple welcomed the children into their warm kitchen and the border police thanked them and left. Soon, Arthur and his siblings were eating hot mutton stew and black, chewy bread. Arthur, though hungry like the rest, would stop between spoonfuls and stare wide-eyed. Striped cats...black cats...gray cats with green eyes. They lounged on the simple, meager furniture and scampered across the faded linoleum. Arthur had never seen so many cats.

Late into the night, after hours of searching, their mother and Bella appeared at the door. There were hugs and tears and demands for cake from Arthur. Alla had been speaking with the border guards and asking them to beg the Russian soldiers to let them cross the bridge, but the soldiers would have none of it. Finally, after the border guards lubricated the soldiers with a goodly amount of Polish vodka, the old officer made a deal. "The woman, her kids and the other two families can cross only by the river...but I must make it look like we're doing our job. We'll fire over your heads... just cross quickly."

Walking down the steep bank under a cloud-covered moon, Arthur and his family gingerly entered the cold waters of the Yujniy Gerzel River. The river, fed by glaciers from the Caucasus Mountains, was ice-cream-headache cold and waist deep on the men from the other families who passed Arthur between them and chest deep on Rustam and the girls. With bullets zinging harmlessly over their heads, they struggled across the river with its fast current for what seemed like half an hour.

Arthur was now a refugee, though the word would have meant little to him. He had left the only home he'd ever known behind him. The familiar kitchen smells, the sunflower-patterned curtains on the windows, his toy wooden farm animals, his sister's cracked china dolls, and Rustam's favorite soccer ball would soon all be a fading memory. He was in Dagestan and soon to be driven to his new country in Azerbaijan. But for a frightened and puzzled little three-year-old, he might as well have been on the dark side of the moon.

A map showing Chechnya, Dagestan, and Azerbaijan

CHAPTER 3

ARTHUR AND HIS FAMILY climbed up the rocky, slippery bank of the river. They were icy cold and soaking wet. Their clothing had already started to stiffen. Only Arthur, who had been carried by the men, was dry. Bella's teeth chattered loudly and Arthur, who had never experienced chattering teeth before, began to laugh.

"Don't laugh at your sister, little wolf," Alla scolded, "Someday you will feel the cold and your teeth will make the same noise too."

At the top of the bank was a group of Dagestanis, friends of Arthur's father. Soon Arthur and the others were put in cozy cars and taken to local homes to further warm up, get their clothing dried, and eat bowl after bowl of hot stew. Arthur could hardly keep his eyes open.

That night, in the strange bed alongside his brother, he dreamed of dark woods, fiery explosions, and giant black bears chasing him with sharp teeth and horrible breath.

"Hey, Wolf," his brother said in the pale light of morning, "You kicked me a lot last night. It was like you were running in your sleep, just like Grandpa's old dog does when he sleeps in front of the fire."

"There were bears!" Arthur said, his eyes wide as he looked around the small room for any sign of scary beasts.

After a big breakfast of hot porridge and just-baked bread with honey, the Dagestanis took the family to the buses that would carry them to safety and their new home in Azerbaijan. There was a long line of buses, all crammed with refugees, luggage, and bundles of clothing. Babies wailed, children cried, and everywhere someone was coughing. Everyone on Arthur's bus seemed to have a cold. The stray dog from the bridge was there as well, running from bus to bus looking for a handout. The dog would stop ever so often, bark at some invisible phantom and spin furiously, chasing its tail.

"You see that dog?" Alla said. The children all leaned over their mother, squinting at the poor creature through the dirty window of the bus. "That dog has been driven crazy by the noises from this awful war."

"This war will drive us all crazy," a very old woman in the seat in front of them said, twisting her neck to face them.

Her eyes were red with tears, and a swollen red bruise stuck out on her left cheekbone.

"What happened to your face?" Arthur blurted out, getting a not-so-gentle elbow to the ribs and a stern look from Alla.

"The soldier threw me to the ground," she said, choking back tears. "I had a large picture of me and my Mirza on our wedding day. A treasured photograph in a silver frame. The soldier said it was too big to go on the bus and tried to take it. When I wouldn't let go, he pushed me down and grabbed it. He threw it on the big pile of other things the soldiers said were too big."

Arthur had seen the pile; there were all manner of toasters, radios, lamps, large sports trophies, and even a beautifully carved rocking horse with real horsehair for a mane.

A rocking horse abandoned in a field

Arthur had stared at the wooden horse and then up at his mother. As if she could read his mind, she had smiled and shook her head. "Maybe for your birthday, little wolf. If you are a good boy, maybe on your birthday."

The bus was quite old, made decades earlier in a factory as big as a football field in the old Soviet Union. There was no heat inside, the windows all rattled, and the ripped seats were held together by peeling strips of duct tape. The shock absorbers had long ago failed and the bus rode on the springs only, causing the passengers to bounce in their seats. Everyone held on tightly to their luggage. Mothers held even tighter to their screaming babies.

The bus had only been traveling for thirty minutes when everyone had to get off at the first checkpoint and show the Russian soldiers their passports. The soldiers yelled at the refugees, shoving them and slapping a few. "No talking," a short Cossack soldier barked, "Keep a straight line or there will be trouble." And to show he meant business, he struck the nearest man in line across the face with the back of his hand.

Many of the soldiers wore balaclavas and Arthur could only see their angry eyes and cursing mouths. They all carried rifles and many had their fingers on the trigger. They frightened him and he gripped Rustam's hand tightly. "I'm scared," he whispered. "It's okay, little wolf," Bella said from behind him, "Soon we'll be with Father in our new home.

He'll probably have candy."

But it wouldn't be soon. There were many other check-points with long lines and angry pushing and shoving sol-diers at every one. On the bus between the checkpoints, Arthur looked out the window at the lonely snow-covered mountains and the many fast-moving rivers, wondering where he was and where he was going. When the bus went around a sharp curve on the narrow, steep roads, Arthur could see all the way to the bottom of the cliffs and some-times saw little houses. He wondered if he would be going to those houses to live. He was sure getting tired of riding on the old bus.

A very drunk man in a suit and tie, sitting at the front of the bus, began to sing an old Chechen folk tune: "High in the Mountains." He was playing a dechik-pondur, a three-stringed guitar, one of the very first musical instruments in Chechnya. The man had bribed a soldier with vodka and cash to let him bring the pondur on the bus.

"Hey!" Bariyat sang out. "That's Alvi from our street."

"Yes," Alla nodded. "I saw him get on at the last check-point. He was kicked off another bus...probably for bad singing."

Arthur knew who Alvi was. He lived in the big gray house at the end of his street. There was a pear tree in the front yard that Arthur would sometimes climb. "You're not a wolf, Arthur," Alvi joked. "You're more like a monkey. Now get down from my tree and I'll fill your pockets with candy."

Arthur was grinning, as were all the children. There was someone from their neighborhood on the bus. Maybe there would be other neighbors...maybe they would see all of their neighbors.

The last checkpoint was at the border to Azerbaijan. The Azerbaijani soldiers also had weapons, but none wore masks, and they smiled and were polite.

Arthur's father, Hairuddin, was waiting for them in a large taxicab. There were hugs all around. Alla and Bariyat were crying.

Baku, Azerbaijan, where the family settled

"My family. All of my family," Hairuddin said. "I was worried. I heard what happened on the bridge. And it took you forever to get here."

"Yes, there were many checkpoints and long lines," said Alla. "Ten hours on that old Soviet bus. And the last hour… guess what? We had to listen to Alvi, drunk and singing like a wounded animal, playing his father's old pondur."

"Alvi's here?" Hairuddin brightened. "Someone to play chess with. This is very good. Even drunk, he plays well. Now, tell me everything."

After each member of his family excitedly told him of the events of the day before, Hairuddin patted Arthur's head. "So you told the border guards your name was Wolf? And you didn't even cry? Well, that ought to be worth something," he said, reaching into his pocket for a handful of wrapped toffees which he dropped in Arthur's lap.

"Thanks, Dad," Arthur said with a big grin, popping a toffee into his mouth. And then another.

CHAPTER 4

ARTHUR LOOKED AROUND the small, two-bedroom apartment in Baku, Azerbaijan, in disbelief. *This can't be our new home,* he thought, a lump in his throat. There was no yard to play in. There were no fruit trees to climb. He suddenly missed his home in Chechnya very badly. He closed his eyes and saw his happy bedroom, painted blue like the sky, and his toy trucks and toy rubber soldiers. He thought of the toy soldiers and how he'd make them battle his giant wooden farm animals...how the rooster with his big red beak would peck the toy soldier with the machine-gun. Arthur laughed out loud at this vision and opened his eyes. His whole family was staring at him.

"What's the joke?" his brother finally asked. Rustam had

a crush on a girl back in Chechnya and he was in a sour mood.

"The big rooster is pecking the soldier." He said, laughing again. Arthur didn't like soldiers anymore...they yelled and pushed and hit people. He thought if he were back home he'd melt the toy soldiers in Grandpa's fireplace.

"Too much candy." His father said, shrugging. "All that sugar has put a dent in his brain. Now you had better wash your teeth, little wolf. There are new toothbrushes here for everybody."

Arthur's father and mother at the dental office in Baku, Azerbaijan

Hairuddin was a dentist and was always lecturing his children to wash and floss. He had a small dental office near the airport and had a good reputation as an orthodontist. Later, Alla, who had been a nurse in Chechnya, would assist him in his dental practice. When business was good, they would move to better apartments. When business was bad, they would move back to the cramped lodgings of the cheaper buildings.

Arthur slept in the same room as his parents. His brother and sister had the other room. As he grew older, he would share a room with Rustam, the girls would have the other bedroom, and his parents would sleep in the living room. For a little boy who loved to play outdoors—to run, and jump, and climb—being cooped up in this tiny apartment was like a prison sentence. A small television only got two local channels and boomed at him in a language he didn't know yet. Rustam and Bella watched it anyway, staring at it blankly like two zombies, but slowly learning the language. The bookish Bariyat was always reading one of her books and was never really in the apartment, but hiding from an evil knight in a tunnel beneath a castle or chasing the master spy in an English sports car.

"C'mon little wolf," Rustam said one day, sensing Arthur's unease and leading him into a bedroom. He took some electrical tape from his father's tool chest and three pairs of socks from a drawer and put together a not-so-bad soccer ball. "I'll be in goal and you try to get one by me," Rustam said, happy to see the joy come back in Arthur's face.

Arthur's very first word had been "Goal!" When he was a baby, his mother would often take him in a stroller to watch Rustam play soccer. When the ball went into the net, the players would yell, "Goal!" so long and loud that Arthur couldn't help but begin to repeat it. When Arthur's father heard about the little wolf's first word, he beamed proudly and announced that Arthur would one day be a champion soccer player. Years later, when Arthur had a bedroom overflowing with bronze trophies and soccer medals that hung on every wall, his mother would remind him of his father's bang-on prediction.

Tenement buildings in Baku Old Town

Everything in Baku seemed strange and often scary to the little wolf. The wind was always howling, the limbs of the trees waving back and forth like they were alive. One night when Arthur was walking home in the dusk after a pick-up soccer game, he heard someone playing a cello off-key in a darkened apartment. The ferocious wind, screaming like a witch in a nightmare, whipped the long branches of a willow in his direction, ready to grab poor Arthur. He ran for his life the three blocks to yet another small apartment home, for once glad not to be outside.

The name *Baku* comes from the Persian word *Bādkube*, which means "pounding winds." Arthur hated the wind. In the winter it made everything that much colder. In the summer, the city's dust and dirt would blow in his eyes and nose, blinding and choking him as he tried to kick the soccer ball into the back of the net.

Arthur had never seen an ocean. As he stared at the vastness of the Caspian Sea on the Baku shore for the first time, not being able to see the far shore, he felt small and strangely worried. The constant winds gave birth to huge, black waves that sprayed a sudsy foam on Arthur's bare feet. Rustam and his sisters all went in the water. Alla put a red donut floaty securely around Arthur's waist.

"It's okay little wolf," his mother soothed. "Rustam is watching you. He will keep you safe."

Arthur stepped into the water, walking toward his big brother. It was the middle of July, but the water didn't seem to know this. It was middle-of-February cold and Arthur wanted out. Much later, Rustam would teach him to swim... but in a warm pool.

Arthur cried when he was hauled off to kindergarten at the age of five. He wanted to hide and not be seen. He couldn't understand the language and all these children were new to him. He only wanted to climb trees and play soccer.

Once in school he slowly began to learn the language, but his favorite activity was watching the clock slowly tick away the minutes to the end of the school day. In the afternoon the children had naps and he especially liked this down time when he wouldn't be called on and get laughed at by the other children when he couldn't understand the teacher.

One of his sisters would always pick him up to take him home. One day after school, no sister came. She had gotten a detention and was late. Arthur decided he could get home by himself and got on the bus—the wrong bus. He looked out the window at the houses going by and began to realize something wasn't right. These were not the houses he saw every day going home. Where was the familiar ice-cream stall? Where was the big mosque with the shiny gold dome?

The Taza Pir
Mosque in Baku,
Azerbaijan

Arthur got off at the next stop, sat on a bench, and began to cry. Maybe he would never see his parents, his sisters, or his brother again. Maybe he would go to jail and be beaten by soldiers.

"Hey little man," said an older lady who smelled good, sitting next to Arthur. "What could possibly be so bad as to cause all this?"

He couldn't understand all she said, so he spoke to her in Russian.

"I got on the wrong bus. I'm lost," he sobbed.

"Well, then, tell me what your home looks like," she replied in Russian.

Arthur described his building and the sweet-smelling woman hailed a taxi and took him home. Alla, her face red from crying, hugged Arthur to her and then took the woman's hand. "How can I ever repay you?"

The women laughed and said in perfect Chechen, "We Chechens must look out for each other. Meeting such a handsome and brave boy is payment enough." Then she kissed the wolf on the top of his head and left, humming an old Chechen tune.

CHAPTER 5

ARTHUR FINALLY MADE friends and learned the Azerbaijani language by playing soccer. In kindergarten, he felt confused, embarrassed by his trouble with the language, and afraid to make a fool of himself. When he played soccer, however, he would pick up words easily. Soccer was played on the cement, in parking areas, or on side streets. Instead of a net, they used two big rocks to indicate the goal posts. Arthur and the other players all took the matches seriously and goalies would often dive on the rough cement to block a shot, only to get up scraped and bloody, grinning as the players from both teams cheered a good save. There was also one word that every soccer player there and everyone in the soccer world knew: "Gooaal!"

Arthur would play until dark, sometimes forgetting to eat. His mother or brother would have to go out and find him. After dinner, he would often go outside again to play hide-and-seek with his new friends. Always the best athlete, Arthur would scamper up trees to hide, often swinging among the tall branches from tree to tree. He had no fear of falling and always enjoyed climbing. He was very strong. From an early age, Rustam would make Arthur lift weights and do push-ups to strengthen his arms. Arthur also liked the taste of fruit...especially fruit from a neighbor's tree.

Arthur up a tree

"Get out from my tree, you little devil child!" the old woman in the faded scarf cackled shrilly. She yelled up at Arthur and waving a corn broom harmlessly in his direction. "Stop eating my alcha fruit!"

Arthur continued to eat the fruit. A green fruit the size of a plum, the alcha had a sweet and sour taste that Arthur could not get enough of.

"I don't understand you," Arthur said in Chechen, taking another bite of the fruit.

"Don't be trying to trick me, devil monkey boy. My granddaughter is in your class at school. I've seen you with your mother there. I know you can understand me."

Arthur took another bite and slowly descended the tree, dropping the last four feet to the grass and beginning to scurry away. But the old woman was fast too, and she gave Arthur a good smack on his backside with the broom.

"Next time will be worse for you," she warbled after the fast retreating little wolf, waving her broom after him.

Arthur saw this as a challenge. The fruit was too good to pass up. He waited for a dark, moonless night and quietly snuck over to the tree for more of the yummy, summer-warm fruit.

After his third or fourth alcha, the Baku wind blew away the clouds covering the moon. At the bottom of the tree stood the old woman. She stared up at him, her headscarf dancing to one side in the wind and squinting one eye shut. Arthur's grandfather had told him of the evil eye and the wolf was suddenly afraid.

"There is an angel ghost at the big mosque. People have seen it," the old woman hissed. "I will have him send an evil jinn to you in the form of a black dog!" She turned and walked back to her house, leaving the trembling boy alone.

In that hot summer before grade one, little Arthur watched for the black dog. The streets of Baku were always full of feral cats and stray dogs. Some of those dogs were black. The dogs were mostly afraid of people and stayed away. Arthur began to forget the old woman's curse, until one day at the communal well, carrying back two buckets of water, he saw a little African boy his age. He was very black, and Arthur, who seldom watched television, had never seen a black person. He dropped his buckets and ran. Was this the black dog?

Later, after Rustam showed him a map of Africa and explained the little boy's color, Arthur and the boy, who lived in Arthur's building, became good friends and played Nintendo soccer games together in the building's games room. *He's not the black dog*, Arthur thought, *just another kid with different colored skin.*

But the evil eye and scary words from the woman still bothered him. Later that fall, on a strangely warm November night after school had started, Arthur awoke to his bed bouncing up and down, ceiling lights swinging back and forth and the sounds of dishes crashing to the floor. It was a big, noisy earthquake, a seven on the Richter scale, but a half-asleep Arthur could only think of evil jinns and angel ghosts finally coming to get him.

His mother lifted him off the bed and the whole family

ran outside—Arthur still in his pajamas. The streets were crowded with all the residents from the apartments and nearby houses. Arthur and his family stood outside and felt the ground tremble. The buildings swayed back and forth. They remained on the street for hours until the after-shocks had stopped, then went back inside to clean up the mess. The walls had some cracks, but the building was safe. The quake was much stronger in the suburbs of Baku where people died and many were injured. The famous Blue Mosque, with its shiny blue dome, was badly damaged and the adults in the building took this very hard.

At Arthur's school the next day, all the children could talk about was the earthquake and how, with the electricity out, everyone had to use candles and eat a cold breakfast. In the parking lot where Arthur and his friends played soccer, there was now a huge gaping crack in the cement, which had to be avoided or jumped over. It made the match harder, but the athletic Arthur saw it as a challenge. He enjoyed lob-kicking the soccer ball over the crack and jumping and running after it.

Arthur started to like school when he advanced to the first grade. He had slowly learned to speak Azerbaijani from playing and hanging out with his soccer mates and now he could understand his teacher. His first-grade teacher was kind and patient with all the students, and Arthur was now quick to respond to her questions. Arthur especially enjoyed math, as his mother had taught him his time tables and he could answer problems in his head. He was an eager student, always raising his hand to be called on.

For the very athletic Chechen Wolf, however, gym class was his favorite time of day. He was always competitive, and his high energy, strength, and speed were obvious to his teacher and to all the other students. He was usually picked first for any team.

Arthur at his grade one graduation

At the end of grade one, there was a big graduation party. All the boys had to wear white shirts and red bow ties and the girls all wore blue skirts or blue dresses. His mother was there and told Arthur how very proud she was of him. There was dancing, singing, and many super-sweet gooey deserts. His mother gave him a large bouquet of red tulips to give to his teacher, and he turned red as a tomato when his teacher smiled and blew him a kiss.

The Chechen Wolf felt good about himself too. He now knew the language, had made many friends, and had a whole summer of soccer and tree-climbing in front of him. Although he still missed his big house in Chechnya, with its fruit trees, gardens, and his very own toy-filled room, Arthur had now started to fit in. He only hoped he wouldn't have to move again. Making new friends was always hard and he knew that new kids in a neighborhood always got picked on. But he was now going into second grade, and he felt ready for anything.

Arthur presenting a bouquet to his teacher.

CHAPTER 6

"OKAY, TOUGH LITTLE WOLF, try to hit me," Rustam said, looking down at Arthur and laughing.

Rustam had just won the Asian Cup in karate in his weight class and was pretty full of himself. He and Arthur would often spar together and Rustam would teach Arthur some of his fighting skills. Both Rustam and his sister Bella were karate champions, having won many tournaments. They spent all their free time at the local dojo. They tried to get Arthur interested and took him to a few classes, but the sport was too slow for Arthur—he needed the frantic pace and continual action of soccer.

Arthur swung at Rustam, who easily blocked the punch and thumped him hard on his bicep. Arthur grabbed his arm and looked about to cry.

"Hey, Wolf, I'm sorry, I didn't mean to—"

Arthur, third from the left, plays soccer with his friends in Baku, Azerbaijan

Arthur, who was faking the pain, then sucker-punched Rustam hard on the nose. In the year that had passed since his first-grade graduation, Arthur had grown in height, weight, and strength. He was now playing soccer with more experienced players. He also had become a pretty good wrestler, rolling around on the rough cement parking lot and pinning kids who were much older.

Rustam, nose bleeding, went after Arthur big time. He

angrily punched Arthur's ribs, arms, and legs. Arthur, though feeling real pain, just couldn't stop laughing. Rustam also began to laugh. "Little wolf," Rustam said, "punching above your weight will someday get you in real trouble. Those other big guys out there are not always your brother."

Arthur, right, and his cousin at Park
Bulvar in Baku, Azerbaijan

The family had moved again, to an even smaller apartment. But it was not far away, so when Arthur entered third grade he was still with his chums at the same school. The neighbors were pretty much the same too. One cold December afternoon, while at the store buying a sweet roll, he felt a tap on his shoulder. When he turned around to look, he jumped back. It was the old woman.

"Well, little devil child," she cooed softly, "I see you haven't been in my tree again. Did the black dog pay you a visit?"

"No, lady," he gulped, staring at the two warts on her chin, each sprouting a single black hair. "I don't think so."

"You'll know!" she screeched in a high voice, causing heads to turn. "You'll know when the black dog comes. Here," she said and reached into one of the many pockets of her apron. She handed Arthur a dog biscuit. "If you see a black dog on the street that won't look away…give him this. You'll confuse the jinn and he'll go up in smoke."

Arthur put the biscuit in his pocket and hurried from the store. When he got home he gave the sweet roll to Bella. He'd lost his appetite.

Arthur in Baku, Azerbaijan, calling his father to wish him a happy birthday

More than any holiday, April 22 was the day the family celebrated the most. Not only was this Arthur's birthday, but
the birthday of both of his parents. On his seventh birthday,
the year before, Arthur and his sisters had surprised their
parents at the dental office with flowers. That day was very
hot and he had celebrated with cake and later played soccer.
This year he had even more reason to look forward to the
celebration as his father would be coming home.

Hairuddin, Arthur's father, had gone back to
Chechnya to visit relatives that March, but was to return
before the birthdays. Life in Azerbaijan had not been kind
to him. Although he was a very good dentist and orthodontist, business was poor and his patients, mostly refugees, had little money to pay him. His hair was now turn-
ing gray, he was very thin, and sometimes he had trouble
breathing. He rarely smiled anymore and worried about
money and how he could care properly for Alla and their
four growing children.

A month before the birthdays, something seemed to be
troubling Arthur's mother. She didn't chat and kid around
like she normally did. Often she would stare into space or
gaze sadly at the portrait of the handsome younger Hairuddin that sat in the living room.

Arthur and his siblings all sensed something was wrong.
One day, when Arthur came home from school, he found his
entire family in tears. Arthur's father had died in Chechnya

and his mother had finally worked up the courage to tell the children.

"He must have known he was dying." Alla said, "He went back home to say goodbye to everyone."

Arthur had often dreamed of returning to Chechnya, but not for the funeral of his father. Now he was back, sitting next to Nana on the hard bench, watching helplessly as she sobbed and tried to catch her breath. The whole room had an overpowering, sickly sweet smell of roses on this warm spring day. Everyone was crying. Arthur had held back his tears, trying to be a brave almost-eight-year-old, but when he heard his mother cry he began to sob.

An old uncle took Rustam and Arthur to one side, shook a finger at them, and said sternly, "You boys are now the men of the family. Look after your mother and sisters!"

Rustam looked worried when ordered to do this and the little wolf was confused and began to cry louder. He wished this bad dream would end and his father would wake up, pockets full of candy and smiling. Then all would be the same as it was before.

Back in Azerbaijan, the apartment, once noisy and rattling with laughter and conversation, was now like a graveyard at midnight. Everyone was quiet and depressed. They all missed Hairuddin badly.

To get by, Alla sold her good jewelry and some of her

clothing. She then sold off all of Hairuddin's dental equipment. The U.N Refugee Agency helped a little bit, but pretty soon the family moved to a tough neighborhood where rent was cheaper.

Hundreds of kids lived in the complex of the four closely packed buildings. This was an old Soviet-style housing project and was mostly ugly, colorless gray cement.

Arthur, being the new kid, was picked on right away. One day, an older boy stole his hat and ran off with it. The Chechen Wolf was the wrong kid to bully. He was always angry and emotional from his father's death, his memories of the Russian soldiers, and the new state of poverty in his family. He chased the bully down, tackled him, and punched him until he cried and begged Arthur to stop. The next day the bully showed up with a black eye and his much older brother, who went after Arthur. But the brother was big and slow. The Chechen Wolf ran circles around him, laughing and punching him in the side until the brother gave up. Arthur later became friends with both brothers, especially the large older brother. Although usually slow moving, he was for some reason quick as a cat in goal and made a great soccer goalie.

Arthur lived in the tough building when he was eight and nine, doing well in school and honing his soccer skills. Everyone wanted the tough Chechen on their team. He still got into fights, but it was mostly because of his competitive nature. The kids in the four buildings were quite loyal to their own building and were always challenging kids in other buildings.

The summer Arthur's father died, the Red Cross sponsored a camp on the sunny beaches of the Caspian Sea for the refugee children from war-torn Chechnya. Alla was one of the volunteer event directors. Arthur spent two weeks there, happy to be away from the endless maze of gray buildings that made up his neighborhood. But while other children braved the cold waters of the Caspian, Arthur spent every hour of daylight playing soccer with the other Chechen boys, and the shouts of "Goal!" could be heard throughout the camp.

Chechen refugee children at the Red Cross-sponsored summer camp in Azerbaijan

Arthur began to get a reputation as a smooth and tire-less soccer player and a fearless fighter. Soon other kids looked up to him and he became one of his building's leaders. He was starting to like the tough neighborhood and was beginning to settle in. Then his mother sat the family down one night and told them she wanted her children to have a real chance at a better life.

They were going to move to Canada.

CHAPTER 7

Arthur with his sister Bella

ARTHUR AND HIS SIBLINGS were really excited about moving to Canada. Starting a brand-new life there would be a big adventure. Arthur knew little about Canada, but he liked the idea of it. He'd found magazines in the school library and marveled at all the snow and ice and the big white bears. There were bears of other colors too and many other strange-looking animals. Canada even had wolves!

He'd miss his friends, though. He was easily the best soccer player in the neighborhood, and his reputation gave him a lot of respect. Kids he'd never met before would approach him and ask him to play on their teams. Arthur felt proud that he finally fit in. Now he was going to another new country and would have to learn yet another new language and make friends all over again. He knew that kids in Canada were nuts for hockey; he just hoped they played a lot of soccer too.

The Chechen Wolf wasn't just a skilled soccer player— he was also the best Pokémon card player around. He had shoeboxes full of cards that he'd won from his mates, some of which were the very rare Pokémon legend and Pokémon Gold cards. Arthur knew that he had to leave most of his things behind when his family left for Canada, so he invited all his friends over and gave them his Pokémon cards and all of his toys. His friends were really happy with the unexpected gifts. They shook Arthur's hand, patted him on the back, and wished him luck in Canada. "When you're a famous soccer player," the goalie said, with tears in his eyes, "don't forget your old mates. You get to the World Cup or something, make sure we get tickets." Arthur promised he'd never forget his little gang of friends and, with a lump in his throat, said good-bye to all his chums.

Before he packed his suitcase, though, Arthur walked the three blocks to the old woman's house, lifted her brass-owl door-knocker, and knocked loudly.

"Yes—Yes. I'm coming. Hold your pants on—Oh, it's you is it?" she groaned, her voice creaking like a rusty hinge. She stared down at Arthur, squinting. "That fruit's not near ripe and will give you the runs, it will. Give you a bellyache!"

"Well, I'm not here for your fruit. We're all going off to Canada to live." Arthur mumbled. "Thought you should have this back." He reached into his pocket and handed her the dog biscuit. "I don't think there's jinns over there. So you better keep it."

"Hee hee," she cackled. "You'll see soon enough. A little ocean won't be a stopping no jinn, it won't." The old woman dropped the dog treat into a pocket of her large apron, next to her scissors and a tangled ball of twine, and slammed the door.

Arthur stared at the door for a long time and felt a little hurt. She was just rude. If it were June and not April, he'd strip the fruit tree of all its yummy alcha and feel good about it.

Arthur (far right) saying good-bye to relatives in Chechnya

On their way to Canada, the family stopped in Chechnya to say their good-byes to all their many relatives. His mother was emotional, and there was much crying and pleas for her to stay and not go off to some new and strange country. One of Arthur's great aunts said she'd seen on the T.V. that Canadians lived in cabins made of logs or in little round houses carved of ice. Alla and everyone laughed at this, and she assured the weepy, elderly aunt that the family would find a nice, warm apartment. Arthur, though, closed his eyes and imagined a log cabin in the deep Canadian woods, with all those bears and wolves wandering around. He thought that living in a log cabin in the forest might be kind of cool.

Airplane travel was something totally new for the family and Arthur was more than a little afraid. When the big jet rumbled down the runway, faster and faster before getting airborne, he squeezed Alla's hand so tightly that she called out.

"It's okay, little wolf. The driver of this airplane has done this many times. Look out your window."

As the plane began to climb and bank, Arthur felt his stomach roll and gurgle. He began to chew harder on the stick of gum Rustam had given to him to keep his ears from popping.

"Will this take long?" he asked no one in particular, taking a quick peek out the window at the buildings, cars, and trucks getting smaller and smaller.

The seat belt light went out and the plane was now flying level and way above the clouds. The sun shone brightly through Arthur's window. A flight attendant, wearing a hat that looked like a Russian soldier's cap, pushed a trolley of drinks up the aisle.

"How about you, little man?" she asked Arthur in very bad Azerbaijani, "You want cola? Maybe chocolate milk?"

Arthur look at Alla who nodded her okay. "Yes, please. Some chocolate milk...and a cookie?"

"Sure, why not?" she said brightly, sticking a straw in a half-pint carton of chocolate milk. She then reached deep into the cart to get a package of two oatmeal cookies. "On my way back up the aisle I'll give you a refill." She said and winked at Arthur.

Alla laughed and shook her head. "See, you've got your father's good looks. Only trouble ahead for you."

Trouble ahead? The plane hit an air pocket and Arthur bounced in his seat. Maybe, he thought, he should have kept the dog biscuit.

They landed in Frankfurt to change planes and there was a long wait between flights. The airport was crowded with travelers. Arthur had never seen so many different kinds of people. There were really tall men in turbans, African women in brightly colored dresses, a grumpy old man in cowboy boots, and a girls' soccer team from France. The girls wore sky-blue sweats and were kicking a ball back and forth until a security guard made them stop. Arthur was fidgety and wanted to kick a ball too.

The plane ride to Canada was quite bumpy and Arthur decided that all the chocolate milk and cookies in the world would not ever get him on another plane if he could avoid it.

They landed in Halifax, Nova Scotia, and were met by a lady from the United Nations Refugee Resettlement Commission. She welcomed them to Canada, helped them with their papers, and showered the family with literature on their new country. They were put up in a hotel for five days and the U.N. paid for the rooms and meals.

Arthur (5th from the right in the front row) and other Chechen refugees in 1998

Arthur with his father, brother, and cousins in Chechnya

Arthur with his teacher at his first grade graduation in 2002

Arthur and his cousin at Park Bulvar in Baku, Azerbaijan, in 2002

Arthur with his mother, aunt, cousin, brother, and niece in Chechnya in 2004

A six-year-old Arthur with his sister Bariyat in Baku, Azerbaijan

Arthur's family saying goodbye
to relatives in Chechnya
on March 14, 2004,
the day before
they left for Canada

Arthur on a Grade 6
school trip in 2007

Arthur's school
friends in 2007

Arthur trying on his brother's boxing gear in 2006

Arthur and his mother in 2007 with an armful of soccer trophies

Arthur with his broken leg and soccer trophies in 2007

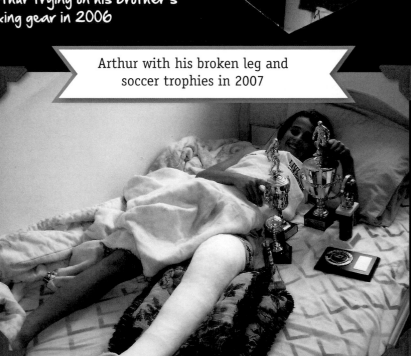

Arthur and his soccer team traveling to a tournament in the United States

Alla says goodbye at the airport

Arthur with his niece and nephew in Toronto in 2009

The East York Dragans celebrate
their Toronto Cup victory

Arthur with his boxing teammates in
front of the Cabbagetown Youth Centre
Boxing Club before leaving for a 2012
club show fight in Niagara Falls

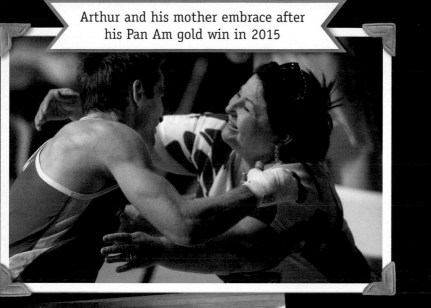

Arthur and his mother embrace after his Pan Am gold win in 2015

BIYARSLANOV
"The Chechen Wolf"

BIYARSLANOV
"The Chechen Wolf"

Autumn, Danny, and Summer Santagato show their support

Rustam, Summer, Danny, Arthur, Alla, Arthur's niece Elina, and Autumn celebrate Pan Am gold

Uncle Danny at a 2015 fundraiser that he and Arthur attended for Mentoring Junior Kids Organization (MJKO) Boxing

Arthur in top form after the Pan Am games

That April in 2005, Halifax was really cold, and Arthur and his family were not happy. They knew no one in the city and were bored and lonely. They learned, however, that two large families they knew from Chechnya had settled in Toronto, Ontario. So when Alla made the decision to move on to Toronto, everyone was quite pleased. Well, almost everyone. The thought of getting back on another airplane made Arthur feel a little queasy.

The flight to Toronto was quite smooth and Arthur slept until his mother elbowed him and told him to look out his window. Toronto was covered in clouds, except for the top half of the C.N. Tower, poking through the gray mist like the periscope on a submarine. He wondered what other marvels were hidden by the clouds down there in his new home.

Toronto skyline (circa 1990)

CHAPTER 8

St. James Town (circa 1990)

EVERYTHING IN TORONTO seemed to have more color than in Chechnya or Azerbaijan. The buildings were bigger and taller and all the people on the streets seemed to move quickly, like they all had to be somewhere and were really late. His family found a home in a large apartment in St. James Town. The massive development of gray-stone high-rise buildings was originally built after World War II for young couples just starting out. The nineteen high-density buildings now housed more than 30,000 people, many of whom were immigrants and refugees.

Arthur had never seen so many new and different kids and found himself staring wide-eyed at the black kids from Ghana, Nigeria, and Jamaica, and at the Sikh boys with their long hair worn in a large knot under stocking caps. There were Chinese, Vietnamese, and many Filipinos. Most spoke English, but when in the hallways with their friends from the old country, they spoke in languages that made Arthur almost dizzy as he tried to understand them.

Arthur with his niece in his new Toronto apartment

"Hey little man, whatchoo lookin' at anyhow?"

Arthur continued to stare at the tall Jamaican teenager. He had long dreadlocks, wore a Bob Marley T-shirt, and had a multicolored crocheted beret that looked a lot like the doilies on the sides of his grandma's sofa.

"I am no to English," Arthur stammered. He wondered if he would have to fight this tall guy and knew he'd lose big time. He wasn't afraid though, and plotted a punch to the kid's ribs and a quick escape down the stairs.

"Hey, my man," the teen sang out, laughing and nodding his head. "All be cool. I be no English too...is no big thang."

Arthur watched the strange-looking teenager bopping down the hallway outside of his apartment. The kid lived across the hall with about a million of his brothers and sisters. His dad also had dreadlocks and his mother could be heard yelling at the children. She seemed to always be cooking, and the whole floor had a thick smell of curry and other spices. Whenever Arthur came home from school, the smell of the cooking made his stomach growl. Soon he would be rummaging through his fridge for a scrap of cheese or some of last-night's leftovers.

A few weeks after his family arrived in Toronto, Arthur turned ten. One of his presents was a soccer ball and there was nothing better in the life of the Chechen Wolf than a soccer ball. The ball was like an old friend and in the field behind his building, Arthur would dribble and kick the ball to the imaginary cheers of thousands of spectators in the stands. He had very long hair and saw himself as a miniature version of the great Messi, the then long-haired Argentine soccer player who wowed the world as maybe the best forward in the history of the game—and possibly the best player ever. Soon his classmates thought of him as the miniature version of Messi too.

Rustam, an excellent soccer player too, would often join Arthur on the field and the two would dribble the ball and kick it back and forth. They soon drew a crowd. Children, teenagers, and some adults would watch in amazement as the nimble Arthur dribbled the ball at Rustam before taking a shot between the soda cans they used as a goal. Soon, other kids would come along and get a match going. Though speaking almost no English, Arthur used hand signals and

Arthur's school

gestures to "talk" to his pick-up teammates. It didn't take long before Arthur got the reputation as someone really special—a young soccer phenom whom everyone wanted on their team.

Arthur went to Rose Avenue Public School, located just south of St. James Town. The school was already 120 years old when he started class in the second half of grade four.

CHAPTER 9

AFTER SPENDING THE SUMMER before grade five at soccer camp, Arthur came to the attention of Bert Lobo, coach of the East York Dragans. The team was only at the house league-level of competition when Arthur joined, but with the talented Chechen Wolf at the striker and midfield positions, the team slowly advanced from league to league to the very top tier in the tough and competitive Ontario Youth Soccer League.

That winter he played in an indoor league and on artificial turf for the first time. His team had reached the finals that year and they ended up playing a really good and tough bunch of players on the Hearts Azzurri team for second place. The Hearts crew from North York had won the

Arthur at home in grade five

national championship for under-eighteens the year before and were a pretty cocky outfit. Arthur's club was excited to play them, and he felt if they went all-out, they could beat the Hearts Azzurri team.

In a very intense game with the score tied at 6, Arthur dove for a loose ball and crashed, hard, into the artificial turf. He immediately felt a horrible pain in his right arm, but there was no way he was going to come off the field—the match meant too much to him and he wanted that trophy. When he held his right hand with his left across his body, the pain seemed to lessen and he continued his win-or-die type of play. It was the only way he knew how to compete and with only minutes left in the game, he found the back of the net and the Dragans pulled off a 7–6 upset win.

He didn't tell his coach, his teammates, or even his mother about the injury. He thought it was just a sprain. The next day his arm was red and blue and swollen to twice its size. When his mother saw Arthur's arm, she immediately took him to the Sick Kids Hospital, where he was X-rayed and eventually got his first cast. He felt like a wounded warrior and was proud that he had scored the winning goal while playing with a broken arm. All his friends and teammates signed the cast, completely covering it with their signatures. He joked that the next time he broke something he'd need a bigger cast. Arthur later learned to be careful what he wished for.

Arthur's English continued to improve in grade five as he took English as a Second Language classes, played soccer with his classmates at recess, and practiced with the Dra-

Arthur with his broken arm plays with
his niece and her friend

gans. He was still far from being fluent, which made him shy, especially around girls. There was one girl he really liked. She was in grade six, a year ahead of Arthur, and had long dark hair and a beautiful smile. Sometimes he played tag with her after school and, like Arthur, she was an all-round athlete. She would even play soccer with him and the other boys. Arthur just couldn't work up the courage to tell her how much he liked her. He was fearless on any soccer field and never backed down from a fight, but just thinking about talking to a girl he really liked made his stomach feel funny. Even though he told his friends about his crush and the girl knew he liked her, school soon ended for the year and she graduated to middle school. He never saw her again.

Grade six was all about sports. Arthur ran cross-country,

Arthur with his teacher at grade six graduation

played soccer with the Dragans, was on the 4 x 100 relay team in track and learned to play basketball. His English had really improved and he had many friends.

Arthur at the end of grade six with his summer soccer certificate

A week before he started grade seven, Arthur and his friends were playing a pick-up game of soccer in the field behind his building. He'd done many bicycle kicks before, but the ball was a bit out of reach and he landed wrong—all wrong. He immediately felt the worst pain he'd ever felt in his life. He screamed. His left leg was broken badly in two places and was, in Arthur's words, "all wobbly."

Arthur with his cast and trophies

His friends all thought he was joking, until they saw the tears running down his face. One of them ran to get Rustam, who called for an ambulance. At the hospital they put a heavy cast on his leg from toes to upper thigh. Once back home, he lay on his bed and Alla covered him with all his many medals and trophies and took a photograph. He thought she was reminding him that everything in life comes with a price.

After the first two weeks' wearing the cast, Arthur started middle school at Winchester Senior School. The cast was heavy and although the school was only a seven-minute walk from his apartment, with crutches it became more like twenty. The kids were not usually kind to a new student, but knowing his reputation as an elite athlete and now seeing him on crutches, the upper-grade boys were all over him, competing for his attention.

The cast was on for eight weeks and when it was finally removed, he still couldn't walk without crutches for over a week. His left leg was now thinner than his right leg and looked pale and a bit shriveled. He was embarrassed to wear shorts. There was no way he could play soccer yet and he felt lousy having to just watch his East York Dragan team from the sidelines that winter. Even when the leg was completely healed, he never went in for hard tackles and his once-aggressive play was not what it was.

Arthur, far left, and his friends from Rose Avenue Elementary having a pizza party at his home

Gradually Arthur's leg healed and he was back practicing with his East York Dragans. That summer, after he turned thirteen, the Dragans won the Toronto Cup, a closely fought game won on shoot-outs. The next summer, his team trav-

Arthur (right) playing soccer

eled to Denmark—the first time Arthur had taken a trip without his family. In a tournament of the twenty-five teams, they made the quarter finals.

Arthur spent seven years with the club and was team captain for the last four. The Dragans won many tournaments with Arthur as captain, but the tournament he most wanted was the U.S.A. cup—they'd lost it twice. As they road the bus to Minneapolis in 2012 to play for the cup a third time, Arthur and the whole team was hungry for the win.

The team chose to wear all-black uniforms to look more intimidating, but the weather was really hot and the dark color turned out to be a poor choice. They won the first game 7-0 and Arthur made four goals. The second game was won 4-1, but Arthur got a red card for punching out a bigger player who was insulting him. He sat out the next game, but the team won that game and then two more before the finals.

The day of the finals was played in rain and mud and the score was 0-0 when the Dragans were awarded a penalty kick. Arthur always took the penalty kicks, but noticing there was a huge crowd, he decided to show off and tried to put the ball in the top corner. He missed the net.

His teammates were really angry with him. As they went into overtime, Arthur prayed he'd get a chance to make up for showing off. With five minutes left, a teammate crossed the ball to him and he dribbled through three players and scored the winner. Arthur ran across the field and slid through the mud in joy. The team then was able to kill the remaining three minutes on the clock. The Dragans had finally won the U.S.A. cup.

Arthur, lying down, and his team in front of their
sponsor restaurant, Sammy's Eatery in Toronto, after
returning from their victory in Minneapolis

CHAPTER 10

IT WAS DURING this time that Arthur began to get serious about boxing. He realized that while his injured leg slowly healed, he could concentrate on sports that demanded more from his upper-body strength. Although he was a natural athlete, his first attempts at the sport ended with his getting the worst of it and he soon realized that boxing was a real skill that had to be studied.

Arthur's first boxing coach at the Cabbagetown club was John Kalbhenn, a former Olympic boxer in the lightweight division for Canada at the 1984 Los Angeles games. He was a no-nonsense trainer who demanded hard work and dedication. When Arthur complained he couldn't jump rope because of his injured leg, Johnny said, "You got a good leg, jump with that." So Arthur would jump rope using just one leg—a very tiring exercise.

Rustam kept encouraging his brother to take up boxing seriously, knowing that with the right training, the Chechen Wolf could be a champion boxer.

Members and guests of the Cabbagetown Boxing Club.
From top left: Tenzin, Arthur, two guests,
Shyn, two guests, Senduran
Middle: Coach John Kalbhenn
From bottom left: Samir, Jhade, Suliem, Connor

Arthur was nervous and had butterflies in his stomach the first time he walked into the club. The smell of sweat, liniment, and leather greeted him. The noise of boxers hitting the heavy bags and the speed bags was a bit scary. Everything here was new to Arthur, but facing something new was the story of his life up to that time—new countries, new neighborhoods, new languages—and he saw learning to box as a real challenge.

When the older and more experienced boxers worked with the skipping rope, the steady beat of the *whap-whap-whap* sounded like music to Arthur. But he could only jump with his one good leg, and the noise from his rope hitting the floor was anything but musical. He often tripped on the skipping rope. Although he was in pretty good shape, the two months off from exercise with his leg in the cast had made him a bit soft and jumping rope on one leg was difficult. Still, he saw himself as a newcomer to the gym and wanted to earn the respect of the other boxers, so he gritted his teeth and jumped through the pain.

The club was only a few blocks from his home, so routinely he would go home after school, get his boxing gear, and be at the gym by 4 p.m. After boxing, when his broken leg was healed, he would go off to soccer practice. He'd then go back home and dive into his homework. The Chechen Wolf always slept soundly when his head hit the pillow.

Coach John was really hard on his boxers and told them that however tired and sore they were in training, the real deal in the ring was a lot harder. Gradually, Arthur began to learn the techniques of the sport and he soon got his medical clearance to go into the ring and box with the older boxers.

When he first got into the ring to spar, he was really nervous. He wasn't afraid of getting hit; he just didn't want to look bad. But the Chechen Wolf looked pretty bad. The more experienced boxers would dance around him and hit him time and time again with their well-placed jabs and body shots. Arthur would feel the sting from their punches to his face and the hooks to his rib cage. He knew they weren't punching to their full power and this made Arthur really mad. He forgot all about the techniques he'd been taught and started swinging wildly like in a street fight. He would hit nothing but air as his sparring partner would laugh and throw a counterpunch to the side of his head.

"Fight smart!" his coach would yell at him. "Fight the way I taught you to fight. This ain't no parking lot!"

But then a quick jab and follow-up hook by the sparring partner would once again send Arthur into a rage and he would forget everything and start swinging wildly—only to get smacked around with a barrage of jabs and counterpunch hooks to his already-sore ribs.

Arthur began to really hate going to the gym, but he knew that if he skipped a session, Rustam would find out and he'd be in trouble. Not only was he getting beat up at the sparing sessions, but his shoulders felt like they were on fire from holding his hands in front of him and hitting the bags. He had many small cuts on his knuckles from hitting the heavy bag. When he dragged his sore and tired body to his team's soccer practice later after boxing, he felt like he was where he should be. Sure, he'd broken an arm and a leg playing soccer, but at least he wasn't getting humiliated in front of a bunch of other athletes who would laugh at him.

Just when he was at his lowest, another trainer at the club took Arthur under his wing. Danny Santagato was a real gym rat—he knew boxing and what it took to get in shape. He worked with the boxers, challenging them with new drills and exercises every day. Many of the boxers hated the tough work-outs, but Arthur began to see the value in the hard training, as his stamina improved and he felt more comfortable in the ring. Danny would also work with the boxers with the "pads," leather gloves that looked like catcher's mitts that a boxer would hit as a trainer moved them in front of the fighter.

Danny gradually became like a father figure and mentor to the young wolf. They would have conversations about not just boxing, but all manner of life's ups and downs. He would be at ringside for Arthur's fights, shouting encouragement and boxing tips. Arthur began to call him Uncle Danny. He became a family friend, giving Arthur a gift of sparring and heavy bag gloves one Christmas. Arthur credits Danny for settling him down in the ring. Taking Johnny's coaching to heart, Arthur began to use his brain to fight and not his temper.

The Chechen Wolf's first real bout was on April 8, 2008, a few weeks before his thirteenth birthday. The fight was at the Ray McGibbons Gloves tournament and Arthur's whole family was there to cheer him on.

Gregory, the boxer he was lined up to fight, was an experienced boxer and was undefeated in seven bouts. At first, the officials at the tournament didn't want Arthur to go up against such an experienced fighter. To Arthur, he looked bigger than the 45 kg weight class—he was taller with a longer reach. He was wearing brightly colored boxing trunks and looked really confident as he danced around the ring, banging his gloves together and smirking at Arthur.

"Ah, let 'em fight," Johnny called out. "My kid's ready!"

Both fighters threw a lot of punches, landing most of them. Arthur tried to stay focused and kept thinking about his technique as he had been drilled over many months. The three rounds were only one-and-a-half minutes long, but as Arthur sat on the stool between rounds, he thought, *This is freaking hard.* He had never been this tired sparring or playing soccer.

Since no one was knocked out, the bell rang to end the fight and the decision went to the scorecards. Arthur won the bout on points, 28–27. To have fifty-five punches find their mark in four and a half minutes of boxing is pretty unusual.

Arthur after winning a bout at
a 2008 tournament

He got a nice medal for winning the bout and could hardly wait to get back to the gym the next day to show it off. But the fight had really drained him and he thought he'd rather be kicking a soccer ball than trading punches in a sweaty gym.

Arthur continued to fight and win tournaments through-out 2008 and entered grade eight on a real high. He was now an upperclassman in middle school and played in the city finals in basketball, volleyball, and soccer. On the track team he made the city finals in the shotput, the 800 m run, and 4 x 100 relay. He helped bring to Winchester Senior School six championship banners—the most in the school's history.

Arthur was named the Winchester Athlete of the Year.

As much as the Chechen Wolf found boxing to be the hardest sport he had ever gotten himself into, he was beginning to enjoy the wins and the medals he received. He was starting to get a name for himself, and by the spring of his senior year in middle school, he had won several tournaments and fought all over Ontario.

In May, in Orangeville, Ontario, he knocked out a tough

Arthur is declared the winner of a bout at a 2008 tournament

Arthur at the Arnie Boehm tournament in 2008

kid in the first round and was now 10-0 with the last three wins coming by knockout. Arthur was confident he could hold his own with anyone in his weight class. He looked forward to a summer of soccer before a bout scheduled for September.

It was a fight that would change everything.

CHAPTER 11

IN SEPTEMBER, JUST AFTER Arthur started grade eight, he put his 10-0 boxing record on the line. He was now fighting in the "open class," which meant he was fighting three rounds of three-minute boxing. The boxers he would now be fighting were taller, often older, and more experienced.

Zsolt Daranyi Jr. was the same age as Arthur and also an immigrant to Canada. He and his family came from Hungary to Toronto when he was a small boy. After watching a lot of boxing on television, Zsolt convinced his folks to let him train at a gym. He learned the art of boxing at Sully's Boxing Gym, where the great Canadian heavyweight George Chuvalo had trained and where Muhammad Ali had tuned up for his fight with Chuvalo. Zsolt, like Arthur, was a dedicated and muscular young teen and had a real passion for the sport. He was taller than Arthur and had a longer reach.

The bout took place on Arthur's turf at Cabbagetown Boxing Club, and the gym was packed with boxing fans from both the Cabbagetown Club and Sully's. Zsolt entered the ring really cocky and over-confident, but Arthur soon made him pay with clean shots that knocked Zsolt back and clearly surprised him. Arthur kept it up for all three rounds, punishing Zsolt with combinations to the head and good body shots. Zsolt was clearly frustrated. He had made the mistake of taking the Chechen Wolf way too lightly.

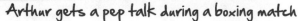

Arthur gets a pep talk during a boxing match

After the bell rang to end round three and Arthur walked back to his corner with his arms raised to celebrate what everyone saw as a clear victory, the visibly upset Hungarian followed Arthur across the ring and in an act of poor sportsmanship, he lost his cool and slugged Arthur in the back of the head. Arthur immediately retaliated and hit Zsolt back and the crowd went berserk with yelling and curses. Both corners emptied and the fighters' trainers and coaches, with much difficulty, separated the angry boxers. The referee lectured both boxers on their lack of discipline and disqualified both of them.

This was the first of six fights Arthur and Zsolt would have over the years and the start of what would be a heated rivalry that would last until their late teens. As the two continued to meet in the ring, crowds would get bigger for each bout. The boxing fans knew that the young boxers were evenly matched and didn't like each other. Everyone who witnessed the bouts saw two gifted young boxers leaving everything in the ring each time they fought, never taking a moment off as they threw their arsenal of punches at each other. Jabs, hooks, right and left crosses, uppercuts, and body shots—the leather flew with speed and precision and the two boxers never gave an inch.

Rivalry is what makes any sport interesting to a fan. In the history of boxing, the explosive fights between Mohammad Ali and Joe Frazier and the wars between Rober-

Arthur signing one of Uncle Danny's gloves at his request in summer 2010 "Because you're gonna be a champion."

to Duran and Sugar Ray Leonard are stuff of legend. But unlike feuds between the Yankees and Red Sox or the Maple Leafs and Canadiens, boxing is a one-on-one sport with no help from teammates. In the ring, a boxer confronts his rival face-to-face and he's all alone between the ropes for the three minutes of punches, counterpunches, feints, and blocks...all the while moving his feet in that peculiar dance that boxers are taught in the gym.

A week after the disqualification, Arthur fought another tough guy, but took no chances with the score card and

Uncle Danny unwraps Arthur's hand after a
fight with Zsolt

stopped his opponent in the third round. Then, five weeks
later at the 2009 provincial championship, the bracket was
such that once again he was matched up with Zsolt. It was
on Halloween night and it was quite warm for the end of
October. It was Arthur's thirteenth amateur fight and he felt
uneasy with the unlucky fight number. The oddly warm Halloween night spooked him.

He fought Zsolt at the 56 kg weight and the winner of
the bout would be provincial champ. Zsolt was at the top of
his game and Arthur was not. He felt strangely tired and at
the end of the second round, Coach Kalbhenn was yelling at
him, saying he was down on points.

"You gotta go hard, kid," Johnny said. "This clown's ta-kin' you to school, so you better snap outta it. Go hard!"

Arthur gave it his all and probably won round three, but it wasn't enough and he lost on points 24–17, and the next day at school, he would have to tell all his friends. Arthur felt pretty low. But still, the Chechen Wolf was just thirteen, so after the fight he put on a mask and went trick-or-treating with his buddies. Nothing like a bag of candy to lift the spirits.

Arthur and Zsolt met for the third time two and a half

Arthur and Uncle Danny before the fight
with Zsolt at the CHIN picnic

years later at the Niagara Fight Club. Both fighters had been talking tough to each other on Facebook and Twitter and the tension between the two had reached a boiling point. Arthur at this time was the 64 kg Canadian champ and Zsolt was the Canadian champ at 69 kg, so this was a bout between two champions who had really learned how to box and win. The fight was back and forth, but Arthur seemed ahead on points, when in the third round he slipped a punch and accidently slammed his head into Zsolt's nose, badly breaking it. The doctor wouldn't let the injured Zsolt continue and Arthur won on a technical knockout. Zsolt was beyond angry and the trash talk on social media just got worse.

Arthur and Zsolt at the national competition in Regina, Saskatchewan

Due to popular demand from the fight fans in Southern Ontario, Arthur and Zsolt met two months later for a fourth time at the CHIN picnic, a multicultural event held on the Toronto Islands sponsored by the radio station. The event had singing, dancing, great food, a beauty contest—and boxing.

Arthur was in great shape and quite relaxed as he sat at ringside with Uncle Danny, listening to music on his earbuds, when Zsolt appeared with his posse—a bunch of muscular tough guys trying to look mean. The match was quite intense in front of the huge crowd, who seemed to evenly support each boxer. Arthur glided through the bout, fighting a very technical bout, and won in a split decision. Zsolt couldn't believe Arthur had beat him twice in a row and demanded a rematch.

The fifth fight was on February 1, 2013, at the Brampton Cup finals. Arthur thought it was the easiest fight he had ever had with Zsolt, who seemed out of shape and slow. The judges, however, awarded the fight to Zsolt and the crowd booed the decision.

Arthur knew that, for whatever reason, he had been robbed of a victory.

The sixth and last fight, in October 2013 was the National semifinals. Uncle Danny couldn't make the bout and Arthur had had to make do with two unfamiliar coaches. It was Zsolt's best fight with Arthur and he entered the ring in great shape and fought smartly. Arthur fought like he was in a street fight, swinging wildly and trying to knock the Hungarian into next week. It didn't work and without his old coach in his corner, Arthur fought a stupid fight and lost in a unanimous decision.

Zsolt Daranyi Jr. turned professional two months later and in January 2016, Zsolt was 5-0 as a professional boxer, with all five wins by knockout. The only way the Chechen Wolf could have gotten any sort of payback from his last loss to Zsolt would be to turn pro as well. But he had a few matters to attend to first—like going all-out for the gold medal at the Pan American Games.

Coach John, Arthur, and Uncle Danny after a successful fight against Zsolt

CHAPTER 12

WHEN ARTHUR WAS in his last year in high school, his coach of the East York Dragans, Bert Lobo, invited Arthur and a few other elite soccer players from the team to a special two-week training camp run by coaches who had flown to Toronto from England. At the end of the camp the English coaches picked Arthur and another teen as players who could easily make it to Division Two soccer in England and eventually have a professional career in the competitive First Division. They told him, however, that he was at an age where he had to choose between soccer and boxing and should spend all his energy on just one sport.

Arthur loved soccer—his first word was *goal* and his late father had said he would one day be the best soccer player in the world—but after a week of thinking about it, Arthur chose boxing. He was the Chechen Wolf after all and he told everyone that "fighting is in my blood." The idea of facing down another guy in the ring, all alone like a gunslinger in a Western movie, was what really made the sport exciting for Arthur and totally worth all of the pain, sweat, and years of hard work it had taken to make him a world-class boxer.

The last Canadian to win a gold medal in boxing at the Pan American Games was a tough, little lightweight from Nova Scotia by the name of Chris Clarke. This was forty years ago, in 1975. In 2015, Arthur said, "Enough is enough," and told the press and anyone who would listen that "I'm going to make history. I'm getting that Pan Am gold." History would be hard to come by as the Pan Am boxers, from Mexico, the United States, and especially Cuba were the toughest and best-trained fighters in the hemisphere. But Arthur, who'd already looked down the barrels of Russian assault rifles, who had learned to fight and survive in the crumbling ghettos of Azerbaijan, and then grew up in the tough and dangerous cement canyons of the St. James Town neighborhood—this Chechen Wolf was ready to take on anyone who got in his way.

Leading up to the games, Arthur entered a new training regimen under a new coach with experience training global champions. The pace was exhausting, but Arthur knew this was what it would take to win in a stiff international competition. He trained three times a day. Nothing else mattered to him. He was totally focused on boxing and on getting that gold. He would get up at 5:30 and, as a devout Muslim, say his morning prayers, then do some serious road work. He'd take a nap in the gym and then wake up for some sparring and bag work. Arthur would go home in the afternoon for dinner, then return to the gym for a long workout at 6 p.m. This was his life and he was dedicated and driven to winning.

Two weeks before the games were to start, Arthur joined the rest of the Canadian boxing team in Oshawa for the Pan Am training camp. There was an assortment of new sparring partners with different boxing styles to test both the men and women on the team. Experienced dietitians kept everyone healthy and well fed. The Chechen Wolf came out of the camp in the best shape of his life. He was ready for the games and could hardly wait to get into the ring.

His first fight, before a big crowd that included Rustam and many friends, was against a very unpredictable fighter from Argentina who was a hard puncher and tough to figure out. But Arthur had watched him on YouTube and came into the fight with a solid game plan. Both fighters started the bout by throwing bombs, but Arthur's will to win and his hard training made the difference and he wore the other boxer down. After two "standing eight-counts" in the third round, the bell rang to end the fight just as the Wolf was about to finish him off. The Wolf easily won by unanimous decision.

Arthur's next fight was with an older and taller Venezuelan. His brother, niece, and mother were all there to cheer him on. The Wolf was always nervous when his mom was in the crowd. The fight started out slowly, with both boxers feeling each other out. The Venezuelan had a long reach advantage on Arthur, so Arthur figured the way to beat him would be to crowd him and punish him on the inside. This worked and his opponent was frustrated that he couldn't get in his long jab. In the second round, he hit Arthur twice with low blows and the Wolf was in real pain. "Don't let him get into your head!" his corner yelled at Arthur and the Wolf crowded his opponent even more, rocking him with uppercuts and thunderous right hooks. The result went to the score cards, but there was never a doubt. The Chechen Wolf again won a unanimous decision, 3-0.

The Chechen Wolf was now in the finals—the only Canadian man to reach the gold-medal round. This was the moment he had trained so hard for and he was never more anxious to get into the ring and show the world what he was made of—to show everyone what the tough Canadian light welterweight from Chechnya could do in the ring.

The day of the final fight was really hot and, as it was Friday, Arthur attended the mosque at Regent Park, near his home, to say the *Jummah*, the Friday prayer with his brother and some of his friends. He didn't get back to the Pan Am village until 3 p.m. and caught the athlete's bus at 4 p.m. for the long ride to the Oshawa arena where he would be boxing.

His warm-up didn't go well and he was already tired from the long day and the heat. He'd been grooming himself to fight the other finalist, a tough and muscular Cuban, for months. His coach had told him early in the games that if he got to the finals, somewhere along the line he'd be fighting the experienced and talented Toledo Yasnier, two-time silver medalist at the world championships, bronze-medal winner at the 2012 Olympics, and gold-medal winner at the last Pan Am Games in 2011. This would be far and away the toughest fighter the Wolf had ever faced.

The tough-looking Cuban tried to stare Arthur down from across the ring, but Arthur only glared back. He'd been

The fight against Toledo Yasnier

through too much in his life, both in and out of the ring, to be intimidated by anyone or anything. He was ready.

When the bell rang the Chechen Wolf flew across the canvas and began to land heavy blows to the head of the surprised Cuban. Halfway through the round Arthur landed a thunderous straight left that put the Cuban on his backside. Toledo's corner was going nuts, yelling at him to "pick it up," while the crowd roared loudly for the Wolf.

The second round belonged to the Cuban, as his years of experience allowed him to adjust to Arthur's aggressive style. Toledo began to be more of a technical boxer, measuring his punches and counterpunching with accuracy. He clearly won the second round and Arthur knew he had to take the last round to win.

The Cuban tried to continue his methodical fight plan, but Arthur wouldn't allow it. He charged into him like a real wolf, pushing him back and landing a barrage of hooks and body blows. When the final bell rang, the crowd cheered madly for Arthur.

When the referee raised the Chechen Wolf's hand in victory, Arthur did the Lezginka dance, the national dance of Chechnya, and ran into the crowd to kiss his smiling mother. As he stood on the podium for his gold medal, the crowd chanted "Arthur!-Arthur!-Arthur!" When the Canadian anthem rang out, Arthur grinned with pride.

After the anthem, with his gold medal around his neck, Arthur ran up the stairs into the crowd to find his mentor

Arthur hugs his mother after winning the fight

Arthur and Uncle Danny embrace after Arthur's Pan Am win

Arthur, Uncle Danny, and Rustam
at the Pan Am Games

and father figure, Danny Santagato. Arthur gave him a bear
hug and put the medal temporarily around the older man's
neck, in appreciation for all the hard training and guidance
over the years that Uncle Danny had given him.

The Wolf slept little that night, on his phone Tweeting
and texting to his many fans, friends, and family. Though
he was just past twenty, he had traveled a rocky road to the

champion's podium. He had dodged bullets and rockets as a small, frightened boy; lost his loving father as a young child; and grew strong and brave in the sunless, cement pathways of Azerbaijan and St. James Town.

The Chechen Wolf had broken limbs playing the sport he loved and excelled at, but after much thought, he made the tough decision to choose boxing over soccer. Arthur, a natural athlete, would have been a great professional soccer player. When asked why he chose boxing, his answer is always, "Fighting is in my blood." For a young man who faced

Arthur talks with journalists at the Olympic qualifiers in Montreal in December, 2015

real adversity and many challenges over his first twenty years, fighting in the ring is as familiar as fighting to survive.

Arthur's next medal may come at the Rio de Janeiro Olympics in 2016. He's now got two new trainers, Chris Johnson and Stephen Hayden, and is fighting and winning many tune-ups before the games. After the Olympics, he'll probably turn pro and might even get another crack at his old nemesis, Zsolt. But no matter what the next round in his sport may bring, Arthur's hard work and tireless dedication to boxing will give any opponent he faces a scare when looking into the hungry eyes of the Chechen Wolf.

Arthur with his Pan Am gold medal

GLOSSARY

SOCCER TERMS

bicycle kick: Kicking the ball over your head while in midair, with your back to the goal in an attempt to score. A difficult and dangerous skill.

dribbling: Running with the ball at your feet while keeping possession and advancing the ball with short, quick kicks.

house league: A soccer league where all players and teams belong to the same organization, much like a school intermural league.

midfield: This is the middle third of the soccer field. The midfielder supports both the fullbacks (the defensive players) and the forwards (the primary goal scorers nearest to the opponent's goal). The midfielder runs more than the other players and must be in top shape.

pick-up game: An informal match on any field or lot where teams are chosen from players who just happen to show up.

red card: A player is shown an actual red card by the official for a serious rule violation such as fighting. A yellow card is a warning for rule violations, but a second yellow card gets the player a red card. A red-carded player has to leave the field and the team must play shorthanded for the rest of the match.

shoot-out: When the game is tied after time has run out, a shoot-out is used to break the tie. Players take turns taking penalty kicks at the goal and the side with the most goals is the winner.

striker: This is the best scorer on the team and usually plays in the middle of two other forwards near the goal. Pele, Maradona, and Messi are examples of legendary strikers.

BOXING TERMS

body shot: A hard punch to the stomach or kidneys. This punch wears down an opponent and also gets him to drop his gloves to protect his body, which then sets him up for head-shots.

bracket: In any tournament, the bracket shows who your opponents or possible opponents are as you win and advance.

combinations: A series of quick, short punches that may include jabs, uppercuts, and short hooks. This sudden barrage of punches keeps the other fighter on the defensive.

counterpunch: A blow delivered a split second after blocking or avoiding a punch. The other fighter will be out of position, temporarily unguarded and easier to hit.

feint: Faking out the opponent by throwing several jabs or light body shots and acting like you're throwing another, then reaching back with the other glove to throw a hard, knockout punch.

hook: A punch where the boxer swings the arm around while pivoting on the lead foot, hitting his opponent in the side of the body or head. This is often used to surprise a boxer protecting against the jab.

jab: A straight, lightning-quick punch often thrown in succession. The jab accumulates points on the judges' score cards, while setting the other boxer up for a harder punch from the other hand.

knockout: When a punch or series of punches knocks a boxer down, the referee begins counting, and at the count of ten, if the fighter stays down, he loses. A referee can also end the fight if the boxer is taking too much punishment or is badly cut. This is called a technical knockout or T.K.O.

pads: These look like flat catcher's mitts and are used in training by the boxer's trainer to simulate a bout. The trainer moves the pads quickly up and down, back and forth, as the boxer punches the pads.

right/left cross: Also known as the "straight," this is a power punch thrown with maximum force directly at the opponent's head.

The power comes from pivoting the rear foot, bending the knees, rotating the body and rocking into the boxer with the arm fully extended.

roadwork: This is running outside to build stamina. The boxer often wears ankle or wrist weights to add to the workout and the boxer will throw punches as he runs down the road.

scoring: If the fight is over with no knockout, three judges hand in their scorecards. The winner of a round based on style, aggression, number of punches, and power punches is awarded ten points and the loser of the round, depending on how badly he lost it, gets seven to nine points. After the fight the scores are tallied and the boxer with the most points wins.

sparring: This "fight" takes place during training, usually with protective headgear. The sparring partner tries to mimic the style of the boxer's next opponent and not to hurt the boxer. Sparring partners are often active boxers, and in a club, most boxers double as sparring partners.

standing eight-count: If a boxer is seen by the referee as taking too much punishment, but still won't go down, the referee waves off the other boxer and counts to eight in order for him to recover.

throwing bombs: The bomb or "haymaker" is occasionally effective, but most often not. It's a punch thrown with the entire body, with the arm coming from the middle of the back. A good boxer will see this coming and get ready to unleash counterpunches.

tune-up: The tune-up fight is a step up from a sparring session, when a boxer fights a less-skillful opponent in order to stay sharp for his next big fight.

weight classes: All boxers fight other boxers of similar weights, and these weights are put into classes. A boxer cannot weigh over the maximum weight in his class. A light welterweight, for example, cannot weigh over 141 pounds (64 kg). Arthur is in this weight class.

INDEX

8/2016